Metal Detecting
for the
Beginner

Vince Migliore

Blossom Hill Books

Title: ID3377772

Title: **Metal Detecting for the Beginner**

Description: *Metal Detecting for the Beginner* is a how-to guide for anyone interested in the sport of metal detecting.

ISBN144212153X
EAN-139781442121539

Primary Category: Sports & Recreation / General

Country of Publication: United States
Language: English
Search Keywords: metal detecting treasure hunting
Author: Vince Migliore
Blossom Hill Books
113 Sombrero Way
Folsom, California 95630 USA
Reorder: https://www.createspace.com/3377772

First Edition, April 2009
Revised, August 15, 2009

Blossom Hill Books

Table of Contents

1. Introduction

A. Welcome

Welcome to the wonderful world of metal detecting!

This is an adventure-filled hobby ranging from diving in a tropical ocean, to uncovering Civil War relics, to prospecting for gold in Alaska. It goes by various names – treasure hunting, dirt fishing, or coin-shooting. You'll have loads of fun, even if you only visit your local park.

The thrill of finding treasure is addictive. Every time that beep goes off in your headphones it's like getting a free pull on a slot machine handle. Will it be a jackpot or junk? Modern metal detectors have discriminators – a word you will soon become familiar with – which tells if that beep is for a real coin, or just a bottle cap.

Although the search for easy treasure might be the motivating factor when you start the hobby, you will soon recognize and appreciate the many rewards of this sport. You will learn how metal detectors work, which delves into physics, electricity, and electronics. You will learn about geology. What soil types are in your area? What kind of rock is gold associated with? Hiking over hill and dale, you will learn a lot about nature, and get plenty of exercise in the process. You will see birds and animals, trees and rivers, rocks and clouds. When you dig, you will discover mud and bugs, gems and jewelry, coins and relics.

Looking for places to search, and seeking help from other people, you will become involved in all aspects of social behavior. You will learn about the history of your town, talk with property owners, and become familiar with grounds-keepers. Best of all, you will find that people are kind, helpful, and generous. This is particularly true of metal detecting club members, who will help you to learn about the sport, and guide you on your way. But, best of all, you will very quickly learn to discover hidden coins and treasure, just waiting at your feet. You will carry them home, sort them out, and enjoy the wealth gained from your efforts. Metal detecting is an awesome combination of learning, adventure, exercise, and gathering treasure. So, welcome to the sport!

B. The metal detector

The main piece of equipment you will need is a metal detector. This is composed of an electronic control box that processes the signal and gives you an indication that you've located a metal object. The output can be a sound, a reading on a volt-meter, a display of a number on an LCD screen, or any combination of such methods. The detector will also have a grip and arm-rest, and a shaft to hold the search coil. The sound output goes to a speaker which is usually bypassed by plugging in a set of headphones.

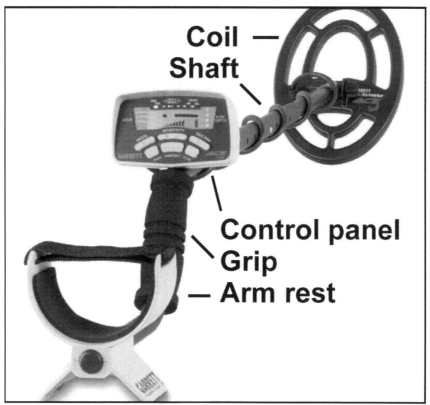

Image courtesy of Garrett Metal Detectors
Figure 1. Components of a typical metal detector.

You turn the detector on, adjust a couple dials, put on the headphones, and you're ready to go. You move the detector coil across the ground in a slow, sweeping motion until you get a "hit." Depending on the output from the control box you can tell if you have a coin or a piece of junk. Some detectors use a high pitched tone for good targets and a low frequency grunt for junk. Others have a dial or LDC display which tells you what the target is likely to be. This saves a lot of time digging.

Extra equipment, such as pin-pointers, probes, and tool belts, makes retrieving your finds much easier. This book explains how to select a metal detector (Chapter 3), and contains a brief description of the equipment involved in metal detecting, as well as resources for further research, (Chapter 11). Be sure to look at those chapters before you buy anything.

C. Code of ethics

The following Code of ethics is taken from the Federation of Metal Detector and Archeological Clubs, Incorporated (FMDAC).

FMDAC CODE OF ETHICS

- I WILL always check federal, state, county and local laws before searching. It is my responsibility to "know the law."
- I WILL respect private property and will not enter private property without the owner's permission. Where possible, such permission will be in writing.
- I WILL take care to refill all holes and try not to leave any damage.
- I WILL remove and dispose of any and all trash and litter that I find.
- I WILL appreciate and protect our inheritance of natural resources, wildlife and private property.
- I WILL as an ambassador for the hobby, use thoughtfulness, consideration and courtesy at all times.
- I WILL work to help bring unity to our hobby by working with any organization of any geographic area that may have problems that will limit their ability to peacefully pursue the hobby.
- I WILL leave gates as found.
- I WILL report to the proper authorities any individuals who enter and or remove artifacts from federal parks or state preserves.

2. What a Typical Hunt Feels Like

What is a typical metal detecting adventure all about, anyway? Come along with me as I go "dirt fishing" to a local site. Everything that happens in this real-life expedition will tie in to one of the chapters that follow in the book.

A. Metal detecting equipment

I've put a lot of thought into choosing the right metal detector. I've been swinging one for a while now, and I've chosen a name brand manufacturer with a good reputation. It's not the cheapest metal detector, nor is it the most expensive. It's a nice combination of features that I've decided are important to me. This includes target identification, adjustable discrimination, and variable sensitivity. I've learned to keep my gear in a tidy box in the back of the car. The coil also required some thought. If the coil is too small you won't get the depth you need to find those long-lost treasures, and if it's too big, swinging it around all morning is going to tire you out. I also bought an old but functional leather tool belt, which serves as a carrier for all the probes and diggers. The belt stores the junk in one pouch, and coins in the other. Read more about selecting the right equipment in **How to Select a Metal Detector**, Chapter 3.

The back of the car has a few digging tools and an old pair of boots which I use just for this purpose. There's a bunch of extra batteries for the equipment. I also found it helpful to have a good hand-held pin-pointer for zeroing in on those elusive treasures. Many of the coins turn reddish brown after living underground for decades, and the hand-held pin-pointer makes short work of distinguishing coins from clods of dirt. Sometimes on long hunts, I also take a sports jar of water, a camera, and a towel.

B. Choosing a location

The area I have in mind for today's hunt is a large lot of empty land owned by the city. It runs parallel to one of the oldest streets in town. This location is on a main thoroughfare created before the interstate highway was built back in the 1950s. How do I know? I searched the Internet for an antique map of the city. For $5.00 I now have a map that shows which parks and schools were around in the '50s, and which roads were heavily used then. That's called research and planning. See **How to Choose a Place to Hunt,** Chapter 4.

It's hard to say when the research and planning for a treasure hunt really starts. That's because, like a photographer, you learn to keep an eye out for good locations. Just driving down the street I noticed big old trees and undeveloped land. This is a sure give-away that the territory has remained untouched for over 50 years. Key things to look for are old trees, property that is free of landscaping, and places that had foot traffic in the past. I generally get up early for a hunt. That helps to avoid large crowds or events that might interfere with the coin-shooting.

C. The people you meet

Before I drive out to the site, I give my buddy a call to let him know I'm on the way. He is a member of the metal detecting club I joined. Having him as a treasure hunting companion has really helped. Not only is he more experienced than I am, but he's helped steer me to the right books, maps, and magazine articles that have improved my skills. Besides, you don't want to be alone in some back-woods area if you fall or need help of some kind. Such friends have taught me how to approach land owners and utility people to gain their permission to search specific sites.

Joining a metal detecting club is probably the best choice you can make for enjoying this sport. People in these organizations are cooperative, knowledgeable, and full of stories that will make you smile. The club organizes group hunts, annual events, and monthly meetings. Learn more about **Who Else Can Help You** in Chapter 5.

D. Metal detecting techniques

I get to the search site, and my friend is already there. I get my tool belt on and load it up with a digging tool, the pin-pointer, and a towel to wipe my hands. I turn on the metal detector, and adjust it for ground conditions at this site. The detector has a discrimination control and Target Identification (TID). The TID tells me if the beep in the headphones is from a dime or a bottle cap, and it displays a message to that effect on a small screen built into the housing. The discriminator allows me to adjust the detector so that there is no beeping sound when I swing it over a pull-tab from a soda can, but that also causes me to miss out on certain treasures, such as silver rings. Read more on **How to Improve Your Technique** in Chapter 6.

Before we start searching, we both size up the site. There are some old trees, and a dirt pathway next to the road. This is a good site that has remained unchanged in many years. There is also a shortcut through the lot, which is well worn with lots of foot traffic. My friend starts searching by the trees, and I take to searching the pathway across the lot.

Right away the detector starts to beep, and the display shows a bottle cap, so I skip it. A minute later I get a hit for a dime. I criss-cross the site with the coil, pressing the button for the pin-pointing function built into the detector. I memorize the spot as I lean over with the hand-held pin-pointer. This hand-held probe is so powerful I can locate the coin even before I start digging. The metal detector shows that the coin is only one inch deep. I get out my digging tool, a screw driver in this case, and stab at the dirt. Right away the dime pops out. I search for the date. A dime minted before 1965 is silver – much more valuable. Whoops, too bad! This one is 1972. I continue scanning. In the first 10 minutes I retrieve 6 coins. This is a good site. Many of the coins are old, 1970s, so there is a good chance of finding silver here. I find a broken watch too, and a token from a game arcade. It's a good site and yields a coin every few minutes.

Figure 2. Besides coins, you will find all kinds of metal objects and jewelry.

E. Science and skills

As I'm searching, I'm thinking of all the physical sciences that contribute to a good hunting trip. The weather is good. The soil is loamy with lots of clay, and it's easy to dig. There are no overhead power lines to interfere with the electronics. The coil size works well for the depth of coins I'm finding. Best of all, the history research and map planning paid off. I come away with 25 coins for two hours of searching, and I find lots of artifacts. It pays to do the research and understand the many disciplines involved with this hobby: geology, biology, history, and electronics. **Science and Your Hobby** is discussed in Chapter 7.

F. Sorting and saving your finds

The coins go in one pouch on the tool belt, and the jewelry, tokens, and semi-precious junk goes into a different compartment. This is the first phase of sorting and storing my finds. When I get home I wash them, sort them into separate containers and drawers that I have set up. In the garage is the big stuff – iron machinery, tools, and farming equipment. In the bottom drawer are the glass jars that hold the various coins. One is for "clad" pennies; those minted after 1981, which are mostly zinc. One is for real copper pennies, and one is for all the nickels, dimes, and quarters. For the really rare stuff I have separate little jars labeled with their contents. Every detectorist knows that in 1965 the US switched to plated coins, going off the silver standard. This makes finding dimes and quarters minted before 1965 especially precious. All the silver coins therefore have their own special containers.

Finally, there is a drawer for all the historical artifacts I find, such as bullets, buckles, and buttons. When I accumulate enough,

I might sell them on eBay. For more on **Your Treasures and Caring for Them**, see Chapter 8.

G. Gold and prospecting

I enjoy searching on relatively flat land for coins, jewelry and relics. Many people involved in metal detecting however like to specialize in specific types of searches, such as looking for Civil War artifacts. Others prefer beach hunting.

One of the major specialties in treasure hunting is prospecting for gold, silver, or other precious metals. Gold prospecting in particular is highly specialized. It uses equipment very similar to detectors made for coin hunting, but the electronics may be qualitatively different. Gold prospecting often involves machinery unique to the hobby, such as dredging equipment and sluice boxes. For more on **Gold prospecting**, see Chapter 9.

H. Growing into the hobby

Later that same week I attend our club meeting. Getting together with other metal detecting enthusiasts provides an opportunity to share stories, compare notes, and display what we've found. Even newcomers to the sport have experiences to share. It's not too long before you learn some special techniques that work well in your area. As you gain more knowledge you graduate from the novice level. See **Becoming a Journeyman,** in Chapter 10.

I. Other resources

We cannot possibly cover everything in the vast field of metal detecting in a small introductory book like this. For further learning, sharing, and discussion of metal detecting you will need to know **Other Resources,** which are presented in Chapter 11.

More resources are in the Appendices. **Appendix A** tells **How a VLF Detector Works**. **Appendix B** lists **Manufacturers and Suppliers**.

3. How to Select a Metal Detector

A. Before you buy

Your most important purchase will be the metal detector. Don't make the mistake of a hasty choice. You may end up with a detector that is a mismatch for your interests and for your location. If you plan to make an informed decision on which machine to buy, you will need:

FIRST – Consider what is possible in your area. For example, if you live in the middle of the Nevada desert, you probably would not be choosing underwater equipment or be looking for Civil War relics. You are more likely to be successful at coin-shooting, searching for jewelry, or prospecting.

SECOND – Study how detectors work. VLF detectors are by far the most common, but you should know what an older BFO instrument is, and be aware of the newer Pulse Induction detectors. Study the brand names and their advertisements in hobbyist magazines.

THIRD - become familiar with some of the tech-talk and key words which refer to functions of the machine, then decide if you really need them for your particular type of detecting.

The key words you should become familiar with are explained below in Section D. They are:
- Discrimination and notch filtering
- Target Identification and VDI numbers
- Sensitivity
- Search depth
- Ground balance
- Operating frequency, or multiple frequencies

CAUTION: A huge number of metal detecting enthusiasts run out right away and buy a detector even before they know much about their machine or what it will be used for. Imagine someone who develops a sudden interest in photography. He spends thousands of dollars on the best cameras, thinking he can sell photographs and use the money to pay back the costs of the equipment. Whoops! Too late! He realizes later there are about 4 billion people in the world with the same idea, AND most people can get just about any photograph on any subject free from the Internet. You don't want that kind of scenario to happen to you!

Figure 3. A detector control box showing the adjusting dials.
This model does not have a visual display, and uses sounds to
help identify targets.

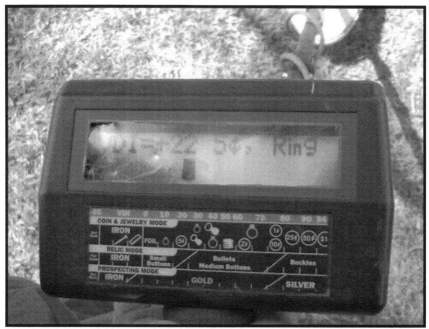

Figure 4. Target identification on a White's metal detector uses a Visual Discrimination Indicator (VDI) number to display the likely object. Here a VDI of +22 indicates a nickel or ring.

If you have the advantage of a friend who already owns a detector, then you will be ahead of the game. Arrange for a demonstration and instructions on how to use it. No matter how much you read, nothing can replace the hands-on experience of actually swinging a detector and hearing the sounds that indicate you've located a coin. Most dealers would be glad to demonstrate different machines too. Try it!

B. Detecting possibilities in your geographic location.

Metal detecting encompasses three broad but overlapping categories. These are land-based coin and relic hunting; beach, surf, and underwater detecting: and prospecting for gold, silver, and other metals.

1. On-land coins and relics

On-land detecting is the most common. Land-based metal detecting recovers coins, jewelry, tokens, household items, and historic relics. Most manufacturers focus on detectors for this purpose. Some brands produce detector models that have multiple modes, so they can search on land as well as in other environments. Land-based detecting includes cache hunting, which is the search for large amounts of stored treasure, such as a jar full of coins.

2. Beach, surf, and underwater detecting

Beach and underwater detecting requires a bit more specialized equipment due to the electrical properties of salt and water, and the need for water-proofing. The presence of salts and certain minerals requires some fine tuning for the detector to be able to see coins in this environment. The coil and shaft of such detectors are waterproof, while some are completely submersible for underwater detecting. Consider this specialty if you live near lakes, beaches, or large bodies of water.

3. Prospecting for gold, silver, or other metals

Metals, minerals, and gold in particular, have distinct electrical properties. Metal detectors used for prospecting benefit from dedicated circuit design which takes advantage of these properties. Operating frequencies are usually higher for prospecting than for on-land treasure hunting As with water detecting, salts and minerals are often encountered during prospecting, which requires a robust ground balancing system.

Many manufacturers produce multi-mode detectors which can operate across two or more of the environments listed above. Some models have a simple toggle switch which allows the operator to choose between coin, beach, or prospecting mode. Some hobbyists like to specialize in just one type of detecting, and will prefer to buy a detector that is dedicated to that mode. A person living along the coast in Florida, for example, may prefer a model that is dedicated to beach and surf detecting.

C. The basic technologies

1. First-generation technology

Beat-frequency oscillator (BFO) detectors are older and out of favor. You might still find such detectors available from old-timers or on the Internet. They may work well enough for a beginner, but they do not have the advanced features found in modern detectors.

2. Very-low frequency (VLF) technology

The VLF detector is by far your best choice for most circumstances. VLF detectors enable discrimination, which helps you distinguish between different coins and trash. Usually they offer Target Identification which will tell you that you most likely have a nickel, a dime, a pull-tab, or whatever. The technology is well-proven and popular with hobbyists. See **Appendix A** for a description on how it works.

3. Pulse induction (PI) technology

Pulse induction is a relatively new technology. This type of detector turns the search coil on for a fraction of a second. The same coil that sent the signal then listens for an echo from the target area. PI technology has the advantage of being better suited for difficult soil conditions, such as high salt or mineralization. PI detectors are more suitable for detecting gold and underwater applications. It has a drawback of poor performance in discriminating junk from valuable targets.

There are a few new technologies on the horizon, but they are not yet in production. The following is quoted from Wikipedia (http://en.wikipedia.org/wiki/Metal_detector):

> "New genres of metal detector have made their appearance. BB (Beat Balance) and CCO (Coil Coupled Operation) were unveiled by the electronics press in 2004. Both were invented by electronics writer and designer Thomas Scarborough and combine unprecedented simplicity with good sensitivity."

The geology of the area in which you live will have a major influence on the kind of detecting you are capable of. If you live in a state where gold deposits exist, for example, you might want to consider a model that is capable of prospecting.

D. Crucial Concepts in Detector Operation

1. Discrimination and notch filtering

Discrimination is the ability of the detector to distinguish between one target and another. In most cases this translates into being able to distinguish between a coin and trash, such as between a quarter and a bottle cap. The composition of the object being scanned has an effect on the signal received by the metal detector. This effect is called phase shift. A positive, or leading, phase shift indicates a highly conductive target, such as a silver dime. A negative, or lagging, phase shift generally indicates junk, such as a rusty nail. An adjustable discrimination dial lets the operator tune out and reject signals from the junk targets.

The discriminator dial, in effect, blocks any response from the detector for targets with a phase shift at or below the level you select. Unfortunately, when you tune out the pull-tabs from soda cans you also tune out nickels and some jewelry. Experience adjusting the discriminator setting then becomes an important part of the learning curve for the novice coin-shooter. Some advanced metal detectors (more expensive) let you tune out only certain portions of the phase shift spectrum. This is called "**notch filtering**." For example, you could tune out most of the pull tabs and still get nickels with careful notch filtering.

As you might guess, discrimination is extremely valuable in the field, where you don't want to spend a lot of time digging up garbage. In some situations, such as relic hunting, discrimination might not be as crucial, since relic hunters will often choose to dig up everything made of metal.

2. Target identification (TID)

Target Identification is closely related to discrimination. Modern discriminating metal detectors can tell you if the target is a copper penny (minted before 1982) or a zinc penny. It can tell between a silver dime (minted before 1965), and what we call a "clad" dime, one that is a composite of copper and nickel.

The output of the discrimination circuitry can be an audible tone, with a high pitched tone for valuables and a low grunt for junk. This is called tone identification. The output is more commonly a meter reading, or a numeric value called a VDI number which appears on a screen. VDI stands for Visual Discrimination Indicator. Discrimination output sometimes uses multiple modes to alert the operator. A high-pitched tone will indicate a high-conductivity target, while the LDC display shows both a VDI number and a probable target. On White's metal detector, for example, a nickel might appear as "VDI = 18 Nickel" on the display, or "VDI = 80 Dime, Penny."

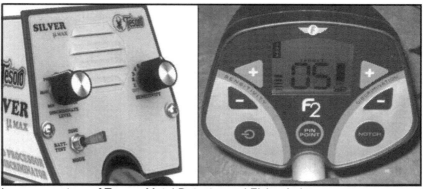

Images courtesy of Tesoro Metal Detector and Fisher Labs.
Figure 5. The Tesoro Silver Umax uses tones for Target ID (left). The Fisher Labs F2 uses an LCD display with 2-digit VDI numbers (right).

24

Target Identification is not always accurate. The error rate tends to go up when the target is deeper in the ground. For a more technical explanation of Target Identification and how detectors work, see **Appendix A.**

3. Sensitivity

Sensitivity refers to the ability to detect metal objects from a distance. It is something akin to the volume control knob on an amplifier. Set too low, you won't hear the music. Set too high and you get distortion and chatter. Most detectors with sensitivity control have a mark on the control panel where the manufacturer recommends you set the dial. Under certain conditions, such as areas of high mineral content, or near power lines, it may be necessary to lower the sensitivity to cut down on noises and false signals.

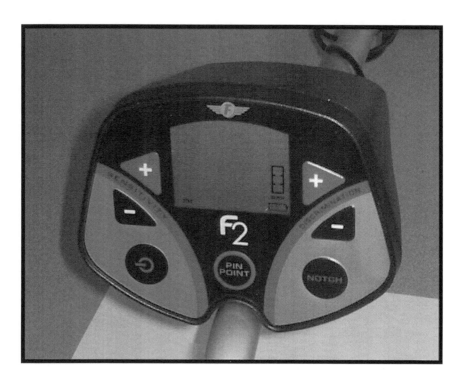

Figure 6. The sensitivity (left) and discrimination level (right) are adjusted with the "+" and "-" buttons on the Fisher Labs model F2.

4. Search depth

The depth that your machine is able to search for coins depends on a number of factors. These include:

- Detector operating frequency. The lower frequencies have better depth.
- The strength of the magnetic field created by the detector; the stronger the field, the deeper the penetration.
- The size and shape of the search coil. Generally the larger the coil, the deeper it can search. Some coils employ two separate D-shaped windings. These "DD" coils distort the shape of the magnetic field and enable deeper searching.
- The composition of the ground being searched and its electrical characteristics. This is usually referred to simply as "mineralization", but it may include such variables as how tightly the ground is compacted, the presence of water, and the chemical makeup of the soil.
- The shape, size, and orientation of the object. A dime buried on its edge, for example, would be more difficult to detect than one laying flat (parallel to the surface).

"How deep can I go with this coil?" The truth is, nobody can really say with certainty, due to the variables mentioned above. To be on the safe side, consider the half and half idea: You can easily find coins down to a depth of half your coil diameter. If you're using an 8-inch circular coil, you'll easily find coins at 4 inches. The other half is tricky. Under ideal circumstances – good ground conditions, finely tuned detector, experienced operator, a flat-lying silver coin, and fresh batteries – you might make up the other half, so you could get down to a full 8 inches. It's in this borderland region, between half the coil diameter and the full diameter, where Target Identification suffers, the signal becomes weak or intermittent, and your skill and patience at detecting pays off. This of course is just a general observation. There are experts in this hobby who will swear they can find coins much deeper than 8 inches using and 8-inch coil.

5. Ground balance

All soils contain some degree of metals, such as iron, which can interfere with a detector's ability to find coins. Ground balancing allows the detector to see past these minerals. There are different ways to set ground balance:

- Factory preset ground balance. Here the manufacturer sets the ground balance at a predetermined level, which they estimate will work adequately in most searching environments. This "fixed" ground balance may be a less desirable compromise, but it lowers costs and works well in normal soil conditions.
- Automatic ground balance. Many modern detectors now employ circuitry which detects and adjusts for ground effects automatically.
- Manual ground balance. Manual ground balance requires the user to adjust for ground balance at the start of each searching session. This is a simple procedure where the user adjusts a setting on the detector with the coil alternately up in the air, then near the ground. Some detectorists prefer manual ground balance, at least as an option, since it provides greater control in prospecting, where changes in ground conditions are important for assessing the presence of gold-bearing ore.
- Mixed or combined methods of ground balance. Manufacturers often allow owners to select manual or automatic ground balancing, simply by flipping a toggle switch on the detector. As mentioned above, in some circumstances, such as prospecting for gold, the owner may want more control over settings on the detector. Think of it as automatic transmission versus a manual clutch.

6. Detector operating frequency

Detectors use very low frequency sine wave oscillations in the coil to detect their targets. The vast majority of detectors on the market today use an operating frequency between 3,000 and 20,000 cycles per second, or hertz. The typical land-oriented detector might use an oscillator at 7,000 cycles per second, abbreviated 7k Hz.

For purposes of selecting a detector, the crucial point to remember is:

- The higher the frequency, the easier it is to detect small objects, such as BB-sized relics or minute specs of gold. Higher frequencies, however, are less able to penetrate deep into the ground.

- The lower the frequency, the deeper your detector can scan, with the same sized coil. Lower frequencies, however, are less efficient at picking up very small objects.

Detector operating frequency is not like a computer clock speed, where the faster it goes the better. The different frequencies are more suited for specific purposes. For high frequencies, imagine shooting sewing needles into the sand. They are good for picking up tiny objects, but they don't go very deep beneath the surface. Next shoot hundreds of nails into the sand. They go deeper than the needles, and are good for detecting coin-sized objects. Finally, shoot a few large tent stakes into the sand. They penetrate much deeper, but are not good at finding tiny objects. They are suited for finding larger objects.

Some manufacturers now produce detectors which generate multiple simultaneous frequencies for the same coil. This type of detector will span a much greater spectrum of both depth and object size. The Minelab Safari metal detector, for example, boasts 28 frequencies. Although this improves your detecting options, it also adds to the cost of the detector.

E. Detector Choices

NOTE: The following is a made up sequence of events a newcomer, or "newbie," might go through in deciding which detector to select. It is presented here purely as an example of the steps you would have to take in that process of deciding on a detector for yourself. This is not an endorsement of any detector or manufacturer. Your personal preferences and choices would obviously vary tremendously from those presented here.

1. The major manufacturers

As a newbie, I first get a few copies of the hobbyist magazines and look at the advertisements. I search the Internet and the online auction sites. I might even go to a detector store and gather some literature. Finally, I'd look at the detector reviews on some of the online forums and metal detector sites. (See Chapter 11 for online forums.)

From that initial search, I make a list of manufacturers. The big ones are:
- Garrett
- White's
- Minelab
- Tesoro
- Fisher Labs
- Bounty Hunter

Looking at the advertisements, I see nobody is pushing BFO detectors any more. They are probably out of date. There are some PI (Pulse Induction) machines advertised but they seem specialized and too pricey for a beginner.

My **First Decision: I'm looking for a new VLF detector.**

Next I examine my finances and make the **Second Decision: I don't want to spend more than $250.** I look at the prices on line. These are usually a bit lower than the manufacturers suggested retail price, the MSRP.

I look at some of the reviews, some of the ads, and the specifications. I settle on just 3 potential models. My **Third Decision: I select top contenders.** These are:
- Tesoro Silver Umax
- Garrett Ace 250
- Fisher Labs F2

They all look decent, and are within my price range.

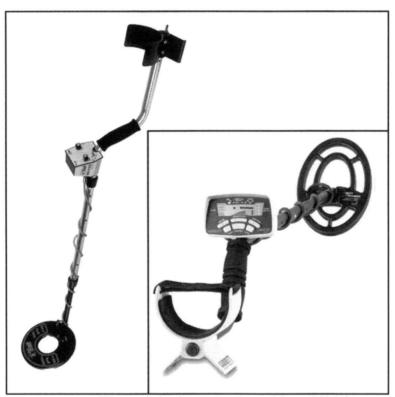

Image courtesy of Tesoro (left). Image courtesy of Garrett (right)
Figure 7. Two affordable metal detectors: The Tesoro Silver Umax (left), and the Garrett Ace 250 (right).

2. Your check-list

Next, I look at the concepts listed in Chapter 3, Section D, above. My **Fourth Decision: I'll make a check list of the features I want.** Using the criteria above, I write out notes and observations. This is from the perspective of a novice, so I'm not yet sure about getting everything right. My thinking so far:

- **Discrimination.** This seems important. All the ads talk about discrimination and it appears to be crucial in sorting out junk from good finds. This tops the list for important features.
- **Target Identification.** This sounds great and should make detecting easier, but I don't know how much it adds to the cost. The reviews I've read of the one model that does not have Target Identification indicate that learning to use the sounds to identify targets is almost as effective as having TID. I will have to reserve judgment on this.
- **Sensitivity.** Just about all the ads talk about sensitivity, which seems to mean you have an adjusting knob on the control box. That seems reasonable.
- **Depth.** Frankly, I'm not sure how to measure this. No one gives any hard figures on depth. For now, I'll just go by coil size, since I've heard the bigger the coil the deeper it goes.
- **Ground balance.** At the start, I thought this would be a crucial, must-have feature, but all three models have fixed, or factory pre-set ground balance. I guess in my price range, that's something I will have to live without. Besides, the terrain around here is pretty normal, so maybe this is not that important, for a beginner anyway.
- **Operating Frequency.** All three models have similar operating frequencies. I don't expect to be searching for gold; not yet. I'm not sure operating frequency is going to sway me towards or away from any of the models.

Something I hadn't thought of is the **weight** of the detector. From the online forums, weight seems to be a big issue. With that kink I sometimes get in my shoulder, I decide to add this to my check list.

Figure 8. Other choices in my price range: The Fisher Labs F2 (left), and White's Prism III (right).

3. Comparing models .

Now from my newbie perspective I make up a chart to compare the models. There are still some unanswered questions, but now I have a platform to work from.

	Tesoro Silver Umax	Garrett Ace 250	Fisher Labs F2
Street Price	$240	$210	$200
Discrim.	Yes	Yes	Yes
Target ID	By sound only	12 segments and tone ID	Yes, sound and two-digit ID number
Sensitivity	Yes	Yes	Yes
Depth (Coil size)	8 inch	6.5x9 inch	8 inch
Ground Balance	Fixed	Fixed	Fixed
Op. Freq.	10.6 kHz	6.5 kHz	5.9 kHz
Weight	2.2 lbs.	2.7 lbs.	2.5 lbs.
Summary	Light weight; target sounds only, easy to use	Good reviews; TID but no VDI #s	Lowest price; TID #s a big plus.

Table 1. Comparison of detector models.

With the chart filled in from the checklist, I'm in a much better position to evaluate the three models. In summary, they all come in at a decent price, and all of them have dials for discrimination and sensitivity. One disappointment is that they all have fixed ground balance. I'm not going to worry about that for this, my first detector.

The Tesoro Silver Umax is the lightest weight. Its operating frequency is the highest. I'm not sure if that will affect its depth, but it has a good-sized coil. Reviews on this machine are excellent, and owners indicate learning the sounds is a breeze.

The Garrett Ace 250 is a popular model from a trusted manufacturer. Owners give it good reviews. The 12 segment Target Identification is not as good as the 2-digit codes that you get with more advanced machines, but it should be enough to distinguish various types of targets.

The Fisher Labs F2 has the lowest street price and an 8-inch coil. The big plus here is the 2-digit Target Identification number that you find on higher-priced models. This adds a lot to the ability to discriminate trash from treasure.

Again, these comments are not meant as a professional review of the value of any of the detectors. The idea here is to make a chart up for yourself, listing what is important to you, so you can make your own comparisons and choose the best combination of features for yourself. You might decide, for example, that you get more bang for your buck by purchasing a used detector. Perhaps you want to consider a different price range. You may want to add different categories to your check list, such as whether or not the detector accepts interchangeable coils.

NOTE: A blank Check-list Comparison Chart appears in Appendix C.

Now, what if you have a little more money to spend, and you want a better detector. Let's compare some favorites. Again, these models are chosen for purposes of illustration, although they are all highly-rated detectors. These models are all VLF type, with round, submersible coils that are also interchangeable. With more features to consider, I've added "Modes" to the chart, as well as battery requirements.

	Garrett GTI 1500	Minelab X-Terra 705	White's MXT - 300
Street Price	$679	$699	$800
Discrim.	Yes	Yes	Yes
Target ID	Yes	Yes	Yes
Sensitivity	Adjust.	Adjust.	Adjust.
Coil size	9.5 inch	9.0 inch	12 inch
Ground Balance	Auto.	Auto. & Manual	Auto. & Manual
Op. Freq.	7.2 kHz	3, 7.5, or 18.75 kHz	15 kHz
Weight	4.1 lbs.	2.9 lbs.	4.6 lbs.
Modes	6	8	3
Battery	8 "AA"	4 "AA"	8 "AA"
Summary	Nice graphic analyzer LCD, "One-Touch" mode.	Light weight; can switch frequencies; can mask iron targets.	Rave reviews, four audio tones.

Table 2. More advanced detector models.

You should now be well on your way toward zeroing in on the machine that best fits your needs. Good luck!

4. A used detector

Buying a used detector can add to the features you get for the money. Just be sure everything is working properly. Don't buy a detector that is very old as you may be getting a dinosaur. The detector should at least have discrimination capabilities.

"Modern computerized circuitry will find more treasure and will find it quicker and easier than even the best of yesterday's instruments."
- Charles Garrett, *How to Find Lost Treasure*

If you are buying a used detector:
- You can generally find the user manual by going to the web site of the manufacturer.
- Check the battery case for corrosion, and clean it if necessary. Put in fresh batteries.
- Check the cable from the control box to the coil. Look for frayed wires or nicks that might compromise the water-resistant properties of the coil.
- Adjust the shaft and arm rest to fit your height.
- Run an air test, or above ground test with different coins and see how the detector responds.
- As above, check the operation of the discriminator, the sensitivity dial, pin-pointer, and the depth reading. Investigate what other functions are featured for your detector.
- Read the manual!

Image courtesy of MineLab USA, Inc.
Figure 9. Another good detector for a budget is the MineLab X-Terra 30.

F. Related equipment

1. Coils

Detectors come with a standard coil, usually between 6 and 10 inches around. After detecting for a while, you become familiar with ground conditions in your area. Trash-filled areas are easier to work with a smaller coil, which can separate responses from two nearby targets. This makes it easier to find coins right next to junk. Smaller coils do not penetrate the ground as deeply as larger coils.

Oversized coils will penetrate deeper into the soil, but they are not as good at separating out two nearby targets. They are also heavier, and may create fatigue sooner than the lighter, smaller coils.

"DD" coils create a search field that is longer and narrower than the standard cone-shaped search area of a round coil. The back-to-back DD coils generate a search field that is shaped more like a fat pancake on edge. This allows the signal to penetrate deeper at the center and makes pinpointing easier. If you have two objects in the ground and scan them with a DD coil, then turn the detector 90-degrees and scan again, you can more easily separate the signals.

2. Pin-pointers

Most modern metal detectors have a pin-point function built into the circuitry, so all you have to do is press a button and you can zero in on the target. Technically then, you don't really need a separate pin-pointer. Once you work with one, however, you will see how much faster it's possible to retrieve a coin. Many coins turn a reddish brown color after being in the ground for decades, making it difficult to sift through the dirt for the coin. The pin-pointer makes fast work of that task.

3. Digging tools and probes

You will definitely need some method of digging up the coins. There are narrow probes, like an ice pick, that can help locate the coin. The digging tool itself can vary in size and length depending on ground conditions. For some locations, you might need a simple flat-head screwdriver, and for others a narrow hand-held spade or scoop. For deeper coins, a larger digging tool is required. Sometimes a sod plug tool is handy for retrieving coins while preserving the appearance of the lawn.

You can buy simple gardening supplies to fill the task, though there are quite a few handy tools made specifically for metal detector digging. This includes the trowel with inch marks to show how deep you are, and a saw-tooth edge for cutting roots.

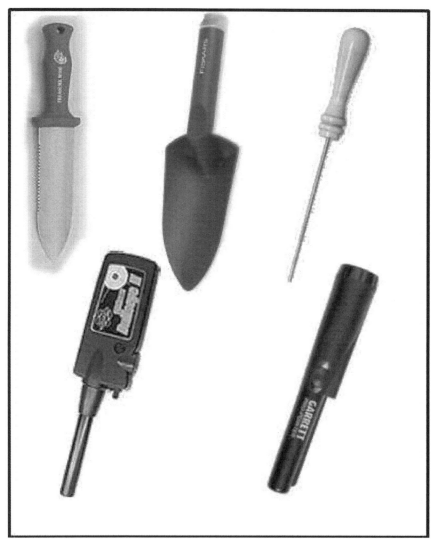

Figure 10. Digging tools and probes (top). Electronic pin-pointers (bottom).

4. Clothing

If you want to maintain domestic tranquility, you should consider having heavy-duty clothing reserved specifically for metal detecting, and you can keep it out in the garage. Let's face it: you are going to get dirty. Shoes are the biggest factor, as they can track in mud, and will get plenty of wear. Consider a rugged pair of high top boots. Do not buy steel-toed boots, as the metal will set off the detector every time your foot comes into range. Get a good pair of long-johns for cold weather.

5. Headphones

A decent pair of headphones is a must. Headphones will save your batteries, and cut down on the annoyance factor for people around you. Don't try to get by with the cheap ear-buds that come with your telephone or music player. They will fall out way too often, and the thin wires are simply not up to the task of rugged activity.

6. Peripherals

The following are some peripheral items you may want to consider. They make detecting easier and cleaner.

- Knee pads
- A shoulder strap which bears the weight of the detector
- Tool belt or apron with multiple pockets
- Gloves
- Towel for holding the plug of dirt so you can return all the soil to the hole
- A whistle or pepper spray for protection
- Flashlight for peering into holes
- Insect spray
- Water bottle for drinking
- Water jar for pre-wash of coins

4. How to Choose a Place to Hunt

A. General guidelines

1. Go where people walk

Probably the single most important decision you will make is where you decide to go searching. That choice will strongly influence what you find, and how much you will find. Search site planning will pay off in the long run with more valuable finds.

Rule of Thumb: Search where lots of people have walked.

Think about it. If you go out into some isolated forest, what will you find? Who is out there? Maybe a hunter or horseman passed that way long ago. Accordingly, you will find only an occasional shell casing, or perhaps a metal button or clasp. If you go to an elementary school site you're going to find pencils, pennies, and small metal toys. And if you go to a college campus, you're increasing your chances of finding more valuable coins, and more expensive jewelry. The key here is to find a site where many people congregated, and over a period of many years.

Figure 11. This unpaved footpath next to a busy street has seen a lot of human traffic.

2. Talk to the man (or woman)

People are nice. Don't be afraid of them. Sometimes, in order to search a site you will need to talk to the owner, the landlord, the facility manager, the groundskeeper, or a caretaker. If you are new to this, the first time you ask for permission to hunt on private property may be a little awkward, but it opens up a whole new vista of opportunity for you. When I first started, I was too shy to ask. There was a street I was working that had a median strip down the center, and I was detecting along the median. Several residents were curious. They were friendly enough to approach me and asked what I was finding. It was only one more step for me to summon up the courage to ask if I could search the strip in front of their house. From then on it was easy. It turned out the sections of grass between the house and the street are much more productive than the median strip. I showed my finds to the owners. They talked about getting their own detector! Just put a smile on your face, be brave, and ask for what you want. That approach is sure to open many doors for you.

Figure 12. A shady tree by a school is a good place to hunt.

B. If this is your first hunt

1. The user manual

If you're like most people, the minute you receive your detector, you'll put in the batteries and run out to the back yard to check it out. That's OK, but once the initial excitement dies down, the best thing you can do is to **READ THE MANUAL!**

Every manufacturer, every treasure hunting expert, every online instruction, advises the same thing: read the user manual. That's abbreviated as "RTM."

The manual will usually describe the factory recommended settings. These are generally marked as arrows or pointers on the dials. If you are getting a lot of chatter at those settings, you might have to turn down the "gain" or "sensitivity" dial.

Next, run an air test, or above ground test. Grab some coins, a bottle cap, and some other small metal objects, and bring them to an open area for testing. You will be surprised at the different sounds and meter readings you get with the various objects. Try playing with the discrimination control, and be sure you understand how that works before you go off into the field. Does your detector have Target Identification? How does that work on your air test of known targets?

2. An easy search

For your first outing, try a "tot lot." That is one of those parks for children that have wood chips or sand in a play area. The tot lot is easy to dig without causing damage, and it's often a good place to find a coin or two. Again, be sure to fiddle with the dials, especially the discriminator, to see what effects they have. When you first start, it's advisable to hunt in "All Metal Mode" which means you turn the discriminator down all the way. That means you will hear a tone for everything made of metal. Try the pin-pointer function. Check out the depth indicator. Oh, NOW do you see why you have to read the manual?!

Figure 13. A "Tot Lot" is a good place for beginners to hunt. The sand, wood chips or other mulch in these playgrounds is easy to dig and hides lots of treasures.

C. Using Maps

1. Working with maps

One of the best strategies for selecting good search sites is to get
an old map of your town. Remember, the US stopped minting
those silver dimes and quarters back in 1965, so if you can find a
map of what your area looked like back then, you will be well on
your way to finding good sites. Try the Internet and auction sites,
such as eBay (http://www.ebay.com). You can usually find an
old road map for under $5.00. If you cannot locate an old street
map for your area, a good alternative is to buy what they call a
"Topo" (topographical) map from the US Geological Survey
(http://topomaps.usgs.gov/index.html). Many of these Topo maps
are pretty old, and they show lots of detail, with schools, parks,
and campgrounds clearly defined.

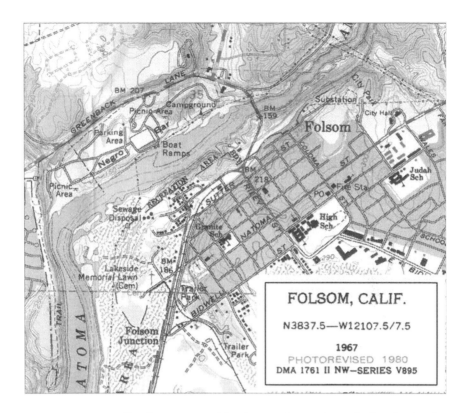

Figure 14. Detail of Topographical map from the US Geological
Survey showing schools, campgrounds and parks from 1967.

Take your old map and compare it to a recent street map. Start by marking the schools and parks that were present back in the '60s and see if those places still exist today. If a school was built in 1960 and it's still there today, then that's over 50 years of people congregating in the same place. That's an excellent place to search for coins. Even if the school was torn down, and now there's an empty lot, that's still a good spot for coin-shooting. If you see a school on the present-day map, and looking at the 1960's map you see there wasn't even a street in that location at that time, then you know the school was built recently. You can still search in the newer school, but don't expect to find a lot of the older coins.

Don't limit yourself to schools and parks either. Look at churches, gathering places, ball fields, and major thoroughfares. Maybe there are a dozen roads and bridges into your town today, but back in the '60s there was only one road, one bridge, and one main street. This is where you will find the richest fields for metal detecting.

Look at the heart of the downtown area where you live. Locate the large open spaces where people would tend to congregate for walks, picnics, or to take the kids. Are you starting to see how valuable a map can be?

2. A personal experience with maps

I live in Folsom, California. It's an old town. When I first got my detector, I found lots of coins, but rarely anything older than the 1970s. Then I found an old USGS Topo map for Folsom dated 1967. Shocking! The whole town was less than a mile long and half a mile wide back then. Everywhere I had been searching was less than 40 years old. Most of it was actually less than 20 years old. No wonder I wasn't finding silver coins! The map showed all the town's activities were in what we now call "Old Town" in Folsom. I started searching these older areas. That made a big difference.

D. Working the Internet

The Internet provides a powerful tool for selecting your search sites. Some examples are MapQuest (http://MapQuest.com) and Google Maps (http://maps.google.com). Be sure to click on the Aerial tab for MapQuest, and the Satellite tab for Google Maps. Use satellite views to supplement your old maps. If a school was present on your old map back in 1965, but it's missing from the current map, then use the satellite view to see what's there now. It may still be a good site to search. Satellite views will also show you entrances, exits, trails, and areas that might be hidden when you are visiting on foot. Even if you are somewhat familiar with the area you intend to search, it's a good idea to check it out on the Internet. You'd be surprised what you can discover. A state park, for example, might charge an entry fee, but there may be a foot path from a residential area where you can hike in and save yourself the parking fee.

You can also find online Topo maps on TerraServer (http://terraserver-usa.com/default.aspx). As described from their web site:

> "The TerraServer-USA Web site is one of the world's largest online databases, providing free public access to a vast data store of maps and aerial photographs of the United States. TerraServer is designed to work with commonly available computer systems and Web browsers over slow speed communications links. The TerraServer name is a play on words, with 'Terra' referring to the 'earth' or 'land' and also to the terabytes of images stored on the site."

Google Earth is a powerful search tool that will supplement your searching abilities. This program must be downloaded and installed on your computer, and works similar to a Web browser.

With Google Earth you can zoom in on satellite views and take advantage of a number of overlays that add crucial information to your search. For example, Google Earth has a number of tabs that will enable you to click on photographic images that other visitors have uploaded. Google is also in the process of providing ground-level 360-degree images to major cities across the US. This means you can see the site you intend to search both from an aerial view and a ground level view. With Google Earth installed and launched, look in the lower left corner under "Layers." Check the "Street View" box; this will provide access to the 360-degree image, if there is one available. All-in-all, this is a fascinating service that will help you in a number of ways.

Google Earth works with another site, Panoramio (http://www.panoramio.com), where you can post your own photos. Once Google reviews the photographs you have posted to Panoramio, then they are added to the database of images that Google Earth accesses. Photographs posted by viewers appear as small blue squares on the screen. Clicking on them will open the photograph. If you are wary of installing yet another program on your computer, you can also see both aerial and street level photographs with Panoramio.

The Internet is a great place to find out about metal detecting clubs, discussion groups, and equipment manufacturers. These aspects of the Internet are covered in Chapter 11, **Where to Find Other Sources**.

E. Historic research

1. Sources

A campground in the 1950s is now an abandoned lot on state land. A former county fairgrounds is now split up into a business park and a little used county park. These sites are prime targets for a person with a metal detector. So, how do you find out about such locations? A little bit of historical research goes a long way towards improving your success in metal detecting.

There are many sources of solid information for finding good targets. Most libraries have a large section devoted to local history. You can find out about the people who established your town, the trails and roads that ran through your neighborhood long ago, and the big social events where lots of people were walking around on public land. Valuable leads are available from sports publications, camping information, holiday celebrations, and anything where large groups of people got together for social events.

Besides the library, try your local historic society and civic groups, such as Lions and the Elks Clubs. Get to know the librarians too. They can be quite helpful simply by telling them what you are interested in. In addition to books on history, try looking under camping and hiking in your area. As an example, I found a book on local history that indicated there was a large boarding house at a major intersection in my town. The location is now a car sales lot, and there is a large, wooded walking path beside it. This is the same path the boarding house residents used over 50 years ago, and it's on public land. Just browsing through the books about your town you will come across important clues pointing towards places for you to search.

Figure 15. Almost every town has a Historical Society.

Another good source is the back issues of magazines, especially treasure hunting magazines. Most of the advice in these articles is timeless. Also, try the sporting, hiking, camping magazines. Look for important social and civic events. Maybe there was a big Boy Scout camp in your area, or a "Revival Meeting" location. With just a little effort, you will find good target areas.

2. Where people congregated

Remember the Rule of Thumb from the beginning of this chapter: "Search where lots of people have walked." The best place to search for coins and valuable is where large numbers of people have congregated. The amount of treasure you will find is directly related to the number of people who have been there, and for how long. You could almost make a formula out of it:

Loot = People x Time

That is, the amount of **Loot** is equal to the number of **People** times the amount of **Time** they spent there. Of course you will have to subtract out the coins that are no longer available because of other coin-shooters, or due to them being covered up by paving or landscaping.

Schools, parks, churches, and public meeting places, then, are good hunting grounds. Most metal detecting clubs will target parks and schools. Also consider bike paths, hiking trails, campgrounds, sports fields, fishing holes, playgrounds, outdoor concert locations, and roadside vending stands. You start to get the general idea. Then you begin to think strategically every time you are out for a drive or a walk, and you start recording prime hunting sites in that big filing cabinet inside your head.

3. Trails and ghost towns

Many locations that were popular a while back may be forgotten, little used, or even abandoned in the present. What were the roads and trails used by explorers when your area was being settled? Are the same roads in use today? Are there any abandoned farms, mining towns, or old airports in your area?

Try to imagine what the roads were like before the highway was put in. Did the horses use the same path that the cars use now? In some locations you can see the old horse and buggy trail next to the freeway where the old timers would travel. Modern highway construction did not follow the same path, because the highway has to have wide sweeping turns, whereas the horses could take a more meandering route. In your travels, keep an eye out for the old roads. Use maps and publications to ferret out ghost towns and abandoned properties in your area. Soon you will develop an eye, like a photographer, for sites that were busy in the past and make for good hunting in the present.

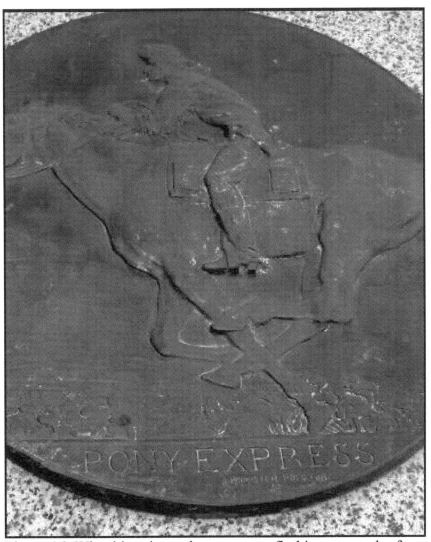
Figure 16. What historic markers can you find in your neck of the woods?

4. The Civil War

If you are fortunate enough to live in a state where Civil War battles took place then you have the added advantage in treasure hunting to add some classic relics to your collection. The Civil War, and the artifacts that accompanied it, constitutes an entire subculture for treasure hunters. There are books and catalogs describing the bullets, buckles, and buttons that are common from that era. The online forums include Civil War relics as a special category. Many modern detectors have a "Relic Mode" to help you find metal objects from the past.

5. Buried treasure

Finding buried treasure or a hidden cache is "The Big One" in metal detecting. Who doesn't dream of instant wealth? In fact, there are books and magazines dedicated to that very idea. Don't get your hopes up, however! There are over 300 million people in America. If you scour the newspapers and the internet, you will find only a handful of stories of people finding a hidden treasure in any given year. The odds are much worse than a million to one that you will find The Big One.

You WILL, however, find plenty of things with your metal detector. Your pockets will bulge with coins, jewelry, and small treasures. Ship and pirate treasures can be found nowadays, but the process is often quite expensive. Billionaires and corporations with recovery ships and dedicated underwater detecting scanners may employ a small army of divers and historians to locate the big treasures. This though is far beyond the capacity of a lone hobbyist with a $300 detector. It's probably better to content yourself with the goal of finding an occasional silver or gold coin, and keep an open mind. If Providence really wants to make you an instant millionaire, then you can trust in the machinations of a purposeful universe, but just don't hold your breath while you're waiting!

F. Unusual places

1. Hiding spots

People often hide their belongings. During the Great Depression, when families could not trust their finances to a bank, they would often store their valuables in hiding places for safe-keeping. Likewise, when our nation was largely rural, folks couldn't always ride into town to store things in a bank. They would use loose planks in the floor, movable bricks in a wall, or stones in a rock fence to hide cash, jewelry, or other possessions. Sometimes, such as with a flood, a fire, or sudden death, the owner would not be able to recover his belongings. Keep an eye out, especially in older homesteads, for common hiding places.

Look up the back issues of some of the treasure hunting magazines and you'll find all sorts of specialty search sites to add to your repertoire. Consider fence post holes, wells, hollow trees, inside walls, under porches, inside barns and tool sheds.

2. Discards

How many times have you been vacuuming, either in your house or in your car, when you hear a loud clunking sound and you wondered, "What was that?" How many times was it a quarter, or perhaps a ring, or earring? Vacuum cleaner bags probably contain a fortune, although few people would go there. Some gas stations now have industrial sized vacuum cleaners, and these too will be sucking up lots of coins. Some enterprising treasure hunters will go to gas stations and check car wash drains and vacuum canisters. Along the same lines, people will search in car junk yards, old vending machines, and thrift stores. The point is, treasure is where you find it.

G. Unusual methods

1. Dowsing

You'll see advertisements in some of the hobby magazines for dowsing rods or remote sensing instruments. The claims seem odd, like voodoo science. Yet, you'll find plenty of people who swear by these methods.

When I was a young boy, a friend showed me how to cut a Y-shaped branch, strip the bark off the top ends of the Y, and then twist them like you were revving up a motorcycle. My friend then had me walk across a sloping field, and to tell him when I felt something. About 20 yards into the field, the bottom stem of the branch started pulling down as if I had a fish on the line. Taking another few steps, the tugging stopped. Coming back again across the same spot, the tugging was apparent again. My friend then took me to the top end of the field and showed me the control valve for a water pipe. You guessed it; the water pipe ran under the field exactly where I felt the tugging.

They used to call that "water witching," and not too long ago people used that technique to decide where to drill for water.

Years later, I tried a similar experiment myself, using two L-shaped steel rods. I couldn't see or feel anything. The big question is whether or not such methods work. Bottom line: you have to judge for yourself. I do find, though, that it's wise to keep an open mind on such subjects. There is a whole universe of knowledge that we may not have yet tapped into. Maybe it's some form of psychic ability, or maybe there is mechanism at work that we are not aware of.

If you do decide to try dowsing, I would suggest you start by experimenting with your own home-made dowsing rods. You can find instructions on the Internet on how to make them, and how to use them. Then, if you have success with your home-made instruments, you might feel better about investing in a commercial version. I would NOT recommend that you run out and spend hundreds of dollars on a manufactured instrument with the expectation that it will bring you instant wealth. That's called gullibility. On the other hand, if you have success with home-made or primitive dowsing rods, then perhaps you have a knack for it. In that case, taking the risk of buying a commercial instrument may be more justifiable.

2. Coin roll hunting.

You go to a bank. You ask them for rolls of dimes – maybe $100 worth. You go home and open the rolls. You look for silver dimes, or any coins that might have value to collectors. That is what coin roll hunting is all about. The silver dimes are worth many times their face value, based on their silver content. The same can be done for half dollars, quarters, nickels, and pennies.

The US Mint stopped producing silver dimes back in 1965, and since then people have been seeking them, so that now there are very few left in circulation. Even if you sort through $100 worth of dimes, you still have only a slim chance of finding real silver. But, since the process is relatively simple, and you can always just turn in the coins again, many people enjoy the process. The best rolls to search are half-dollar coins, as there are so few in circulation, and historically people have not been as actively seeking them for their silver content. As with dimes, half dollars changed from 90% silver to a copper laminate, or "clad" coin, in 1965. Fortunately for collectors, the Kennedy half dollar continued to contain silver, at 40%, between 1965 and 1970.

Quoting from Wikipedia:
(http://en.wikipedia.org/wiki/Half_dollar_(United_States_coin)

> "The value of silver had risen by 1962-63 to the point that it became worthwhile to melt down U.S. coins for their bullion value. U.S. Silver coins (those of ten cent value and above, which contained 90% silver through 1964) began to disappear from circulation, leading the United States to change to layered composition coins made of a copper core laminated between two cupro-nickel outer faces for the 1965 - present coinage years. The Kennedy half-dollar design, however, continued to be minted in a 40% silver-clad composition from 1965–1970."

If you decide you want to try your hand at coin roll hunting, be sure to read the literature and the online forums, as there are important exceptions to the general guidelines described above. You will also want to become familiar with the various coin dates, mint marks, and relative value of the denominations you will be searching.

3. Magnetics

Some science supply catalogs sell large magnets encased in rubber that you can tie a string to and dip in the water from a bridge. Every once in a while you might find something with that method, either from a dock, the side of a pond, or even in the ocean. Nowadays, you can purchase very powerful rare earth magnets that are capable of hauling in many pounds of junk. Err! . . . Make that treasure. Enterprising people will sometimes make a long rack of such magnets and drag it across a field to pick up iron objects. This does not work with most coins, but it is good for the metals that are attracted to magnets. This includes meteorites too. Magnets mounted on a bar behind a jeep will effectively retrieve meteorites in a "strewn field," which is a location where a meteorite is known to have broken up.

5. Who Else Can Help You

A. When you're hunting alone

You're never really alone. No matter where you go there will be a land owner, a park ranger, a groundskeeper, or a neighbor who has a legitimate interest in what you are doing. There's an unfortunate tendency to think these people will somehow interfere with your treasure hunting, but the fact is they are valuable assets in your quest, and the right attitude will pay off in big rewards.

As an example, when I first started hunting, I was wary of strangers, but I had gone to a park with another treasure hunter from the club. Rather than shy away from the park maintenance man, my friend ambled up to him and explained what we were looking for. The park worker was very cooperative and he pointed out the location where a private home was once located on the park lands. The house had burned down many years ago, and he showed us the location. We found a number of old coins, artifacts, and household items thanks to his friendliness.

Develop a friendly disposition yourself, and interact cordially with other people you come across. Very rarely will you encounter any hostility. The norm is to spark the curiosity of the people you meet. With just a little effort on your part, you can turn the situation to your advantage.

B. Owners – getting permission

You need permission to hunt on private land. Getting that permission is easier than you think. You can knock on doors, leave a card, or even send a letter to the owner of a place you think is good for hunting. Some treasure hunters offer to turn over any jewelry they find to the owner, while the hunter keeps all the coins. Be sure to protect their property and refill the holes from digging.

C. Working with partners

There's power in numbers. Hunting with a partner has several advantages. There may be safety concerns, or if one of you gets injured, it's great to have a helper. One detectorist is generally more experienced than the other, and they can help each other. One detector or coil may provide a second opinion on whether or not to dig a target.

Some of the advantages of working with a partner:
- You save on gas.
- It's safer.
- You have someone to bounce ideas off of with regards to location, strategy, and techniques.
- The other guy will usually have the towel, the band aid, or the digging tool that you forgot.
- Someone is there to say "Oh, nice find!"

D. Metal detecting clubs

1. Joining a local club

Just about every area of the country has a metal detecting club. These are great places to meet hunting buddies and participate in group activities. Joining a local club is an excellent way to advance your enjoyment of this hobby. Generally clubs have discounts on detecting equipment, instruction and education from seasoned veterans, and opportunities for group hunts. You will easily make new friends and have people to call if you want a companion to go out detecting with.

For a club in your local area, see any of the links below. You can also try a search on the Internet using the keywords of your home town and the words "metal detecting club."

- Go Metal Detecting: http://gometaldetecting.com/links-clubs.htm
- Kelly Co.:   http://www.kellycodetectors.com/clubs/
- DMOZ Open Directory: http://www.dmoz.org/Recreation/Outdoors/Metal_Detecting/Organizations/
- Friendly Forum: http://metaldetectingforum.com/showthread.php?t=14013
- Lost Treasure: http://losttreasure.com/clubs/index07.cfm

Figure 17. Joining a club multiplies your fun.

2. National clubs

The major national organizations are listed below. There are also some excellent suggestions in Chapter 11, **Where to find other resources**.

The American Metal Detecting Association is found at: http://www.amdaonline.net/.

> "Welcome to the American Metal Detecting Association Online. This website is our newest tool to keep detectorists and small-scale miners up to date on issues that may affect you as a hobbyist. The News Flash page is a treasure trove of information of new issues and even some old ones. You will without a doubt want to check out the Hunt & Events page where you can get all the latest details about upcoming AMDA events."

The Federation of Metal Detector and Archaeological Clubs (FMDAC)

Their website is: http://www.fmdac.org/.

"The Federation of Metal Detector and Archaeological Clubs (FMDAC) was organized in 1984 as a legislative and educational organization to help combat the negative publicity related to the hobby."

FMDAC Purpose

- To unite, promote and encourage the establishment of metal detecting clubs.
- To preserve the sport / hobby of recreational metal detecting and prospecting.
- To make available to FMDAC clubs and Independent members information pertaining to the hobby and to keep members informed as to active legislation

World Wide Association of Treasure Seekers

Their website is: http://www.wwats.org/.

"Our Mission Statement: Preserve, Promote and Protect the right to the use of the Land and Natural Resources for "We the People" now and in the future."

E. Club hunts

Club hunts are group activities. Some club hunts are regularly scheduled trips to local parks, schools, and public lands. Others have seeded hunts where coins and tokens are hidden in a defined area and club members search them out. Still other hunts may be annual events where there is a combination of activities and prizes are given away based on what you find. All-in-all, these activities are loads of fun and provide interesting opportunities for the treasure hunter.

Figure 18. A club member shows a newcomer some of the finer points of using a detector.

6.   How to Improve Your Technique

You *will* find lots of little treasures. That's easy. The trick, though, is to find lots of coins, valuable jewelry, and precious historic relics, and to find them in an efficient and timely manner. The paragraphs that follow will, hopefully, help you improve your treasure hunting techniques, to improve the amount and quality of the things you find.

A. Site selection

1. Go where the coins are

Good site selection improves your treasure hunting. Most of the stories in treasure hunting magazines involve tricks, hints, and techniques to find good locations to hunt. Use your brain to figure out hot spots in your area. Sure, parks and schools are usually good, but what about that strip of grass between the sidewalk and the curb in the old section of town? What about the old site where the county fairgrounds used to be back in the 1950s?

Go where people have congregated in the past, where they lived, where they walked, played, and picnicked. I'll repeat the Rule of Thumb from the beginning of Chapter 4: "Search where lots of people have walked."

Hint: Every time you go out for a hunt, make a record of the coins you found and their dates. Circle the ones that are earlier than 1965, when silver coins were still being minted. In a few months you'll have a record of the best digging sites in your area.

Finally, check out old copies of the metal detecting magazines. Sometimes just reading the titles of the articles will give you clues on where to hunt.

2. A note on the "virgin site"

Soon after you start detecting you will come across what we call a "virgin site." This is an area that has not been searched by anyone with a metal detector, or at least not in the recent past. You can tell you're on a virgin site when you start finding lots of coins and little treasures, and many of the coins are right on the surface. If you're lucky, and this occurs on a high traffic site, you are sure to bring home a good amount of treasure. The key here is to take your time and search thoroughly. It's better to cover 10 square feet carefully than to race across 30 square feet haphazardly. You can then make a note of the exact location you have searched, and come back later and cover the rest of the area.

B. Site evaluation

Once you have selected an area to search, take a few minutes to size it up. Where are the oldest trees? Is this a place where folks would relax in the shade on a sunny day? Is the area covered with sod? Landscaping and new grass can add several inches to the ground, making it more difficult to dig down to where the older coins are located. Is there an area that has not been landscaped?

Look at how people enter and exit the site. When I go on a group hunt to a school, everyone seems to prefer searching the ball field. Maybe half the students are ever on the ball field, but 100% of them use the main entry and exit, and there is a grassy area right next to both entrances. That will have the most treasure. Where do people walk? A woman with a baby carriage is going to be on a flat, straight path, not on a steep hillside. Where would kids play in this area? Maybe they are drawn to that low-hanging branch, or that prominent boulder.

C. Equipment and settings

Remember to adjust the settings on your detector every time you go out. Read your User Manual again. Some sites have electrical interference and you might have to lower the sensitivity. Some places have lots of junk which may require setting the discrimination dial to a different level.

Develop your skill in adjusting the discrimination dial. When the discriminator is set to a low value, you will eliminate junk metals. As you tune it higher you will reject signals from those pesky aluminum pull-tabs, but you will begin to lose important jewelry items as well. It is the mid-range discrimination level that is difficult to fathom. An expert on the subject says:

> "Because gold and aluminum, which fall in this mid-range, are so close in conductivity it's virtually impossible to reject one without rejecting the other. This means that some gold rings and gold coins will be eliminated if you set your disc control to reject aluminum."
> - Dick Stout, *The New Metal Detecting; the Hobby*

One solution is to keep the discrimination setting low, so you accept aluminum targets, then you can decide on a case-by-case basis if you think this location is full or junk, or if there is a good chance of jewelry being located there.

Learn to recognize the sounds your detector makes. You've probably noticed by now that a coin generally has a solid and repeatable signal, whereas junk gives a broken, clipped sound that changes every time you scan it. Pull-tabs are asymmetrical. They give one reading when you first scan it, and the signal will then change when you turn 90 degrees.

Consider what you are finding too. If there is a lot of trash in the area, maybe you want to consider a smaller coil, so you can pin-point the good stuff. Maybe the coins are all deep, and you need a larger coil. You may benefit from a hand-held pin-pointer. Some hand-held units are very sensitive and will make short work of retrieving the coins your detector discovers.

D. Grids and micro-site selection

When you get to a site, set up a grid system or some other method that ensures you're not covering the same area twice. On a playground, for example, you might want to circle around the perimeter, and work your way inward.

If you are searching a baseball field, where would you search first? Where would most spectators congregate? Maybe it's behind home plate, or perhaps between home plate and first base. Where is the grass matted down and worn away by the traffic? Soon, you'll get into a habit of assessing where to search for your best chances of finding coins.

E. Digging

Soil conditions and the depth of coins will generally determine what kind of digging tools you'll need. Some locations require just a probe and a screwdriver. Others may require a small hand shovel, while really old relics could demand a spade or post-hole digger.

Bring the right equipment. Be sure to protect the integrity of lawns. For pristine grass, most experts recommend the flap method, where you use your spade to cut out three sides of plug of grass, flip it out, search with a pin-pointer for the coin, then flip it back. Many hobbyists use an old towel, and they let the plug of dirt fall onto the towel, so that when you fill the hole back up, you don't have to scrape all the crumbs that have fallen on the blades of grass.

CAUTION: Never stick your hand into the hole you are digging to feel around. Often the "coin" is a piece of jagged metal, and you can suffer a nasty cut quite easily. Instead, use your digging tool to bring the material to the surface.

F. When to give up

Sometimes you get a good signal and you cannot find the coin. Soon, if you're like most of us, you'll have a foot-wide cavern going down 18 inches and still nothing to show for it. Such excavations not only destroy property, but waste a lot of valuable time, when the target might be just an old sprinkler head or some other junk. Try to avoid that. Give yourself permission to stop digging and move on.

G. Field storage

Many hobbyists use a tool belt or multi-pocket apron to store their collections while in the field. It pays to have one pocket for coins and another for trash, or larger items. You may want multiple small pockets to sort your finds until you get home. Many searchers bring along a small water bottle with soapy water as a kind of rough cleaning even before they get home. Make sure there are no holes in your pocket!

7. Science and Your Hobby

Science helps you with treasure hunting. You WILL be gaining scientific knowledge, before, during, and after your hunts in the field. You will learn about the weather, soil types, biology, physics, and electronics. All these sciences play a role in your hobby. Best of all, you will learn to enjoy science, as it provides direct help for you in finding treasures.

A. Archeology

Archeologists don't simply dig holes. They learn about the history of what they are looking for. They select a site then painstakingly establish a grid pattern for searching, with strings to mark the borders of each grid square. They record how deep they dig with each level of searching. You can see how such disciplined searching can teach a thing or two to treasure hunters. Such techniques come in handy when you know the site you are searching is going to contain some valuable artifacts.

If this study strikes your fancy, you might want to check out the American Society for Amateur Archeology (http://asaa-persimmonpress.com/), which published *The Amateur Archeologist*.

B. Geology

The first thing you'll learn detecting is the soil type in your area. It may be sandy, loamy, hard-pack clay, or highly mineralized gravel. This affects your digging and your detector settings. Soon you'll be tracking where erosion occurs, where sedimentation is covering up coins, and where salt deposits are affecting your detector.

Geology is particularly important in prospecting for gold, as gold often occurs along with quartz, and you will need to learn where the quartz deposits are. Gold is also quite heavy, and will sink to the bedrock. You'll learn to keep an eye out for bedrock outcroppings.

For more information, see the Amateur Geologist website (https://www.amateurgeologist.com/). They feature a series of popular books which you may have seen. They are entitled *Roadside Geology for* (your state), or *Geology Underfoot for* (your state). *Try also A Field Manual for the Amateur Geologist* by Alan M. Cvancara.

C. Biology

Every time you dig a hole you will come across insects, worms, larval cocoons, and germinating seeds in the ground. You will start to recognize tree types, vegetation (especially poison oak, poison ivy!), and the birds. You will see tiny trails in the grass where the rodents run, and where the deer wander. You know, it becomes a joy!

The field of biology encompasses vast areas of knowledge, from trees and plants to bugs, birds, and beasts of the field. One of the most rewarding aspects of treasure hunting is having the chance to get out into nature and see all the wildlife. You might enjoy learning the names of birds in your area, or the types of trees. The National Audubon Society has a number of excellent field guides on plants and birds. Visit the nature section of your local bookstore or library to find good reference books.

Figure 19. Estimating the age of a tree will provide clues to how old the search site is.

D. Meteorology

Funny, but you find yourself watching the weather channel when you are a treasure hunter. You learn about cloud types and which cloud formations forecast rain. You learn that birds sitting on the wires indicate a low pressure system is moving in. You certainly learn to appreciate the wind-chill factor.

For further information, try: ***Weather*** (A Golden Guide from St. Martin's Press) by Paul E. Lehr, R. Will Burnett, Herbert S. Zim, and Harry McKnaught. You might be interested too in the many affordable weather kits you can buy for your home. They will tell you temperature, wind speed, relative humidity, and barometric pressure.

E. Electronics

Physics, electronics, electromagnetism . . . these are all part and parcel of understanding how your detector works. It explains how an electromagnetic field interacts with the ground and with coins. You will learn about coil types, wave patterns, VLF radio frequencies, battery life, and headphone impedance. These are skills that will help you in other areas of your life too.

As with biology, electricity and electronics is a broad science. One of the best places to start is with ham radio's Amateur Radio Relay League (ARRL). They publish a number of books on radio and how circuits work. See, for example, the *ARRL Ham Radio License Manual*: All You Need to Become an Amateur Radio Operator by the American Radio Relay League.

F. Physical fitness

Being out in the field for hours will improve your health. The doctor might ask you to do 100 deep knee bends a day, and you wouldn't do it, but go out metal detecting and you'll do twice that number in just a short time. You will get more exercise, fresh air, and muscle tone than you'll get at an indoor gym. You'll learn to eat foods that sustain you on a long treasure hunt, and you'll be having fun while gaining stamina.

Figure 20. Hiking in the woods builds stamina and helps you appreciate nature.

8. Your Treasures and Caring for Them

A. Coins

1. Rough cleaning

Treat your coins carefully, even as you retrieve them. Most coins have only their face value, but as any coin-shooter knows, we find lots of older coins, and plenty of relatively rare ones. These more valuable treasures will lose much of their numismatic value if you have scratches on them made from your digging tools. Even rubbing the dirt off as you hold the coin between your fingers is enough to degrade them with scratches. One of the hardest substances on earth is silica, the main ingredient of sand and sandpaper, and rubbing dirt on the coin will leave visible marks.

Just dust off the coin lightly and put it in your pouch. Some hobbyists carry a plastic bottle with soapy water and put the coins in there to soak until they get home. Once you're back home rinse the dirt off in running water. Many people use one of those kitchen sponges that have a plastic scouring pad on them. That plastic will not scratch the metal, and it is good for getting off the loose gunk.

2. Major cleaning

Rule of Thumb: **DO NOT CLEAN YOUR COINS!** Cleaning will remove the luster and make them less valuable to collectors. Once you've done the basic steps to remove loose dirt, you should be able to tell whether or not the coins are valuable. Some collectors, just for the sake of appearance, like to clean these less valuable coins.

If you decide you DO want to clean them, keep the different denominations separate as you process them. That is, sort them into groups of copper pennies (prior to 1982), clad pennies, nickels, dimes, and quarters. Let them soak in white vinegar. Again, you can use a kitchen sponge with a soft plastic scouring pad to remove stubborn stains. Sometimes you will have to soak them for hours. Once clean, give them a thorough rinse in water.

Figure 21. Found coins have stains and tarnish, but cleaning can decrease their value for collectors.

3. Recording and cataloging

Consider keeping a record of the coins you find. Write down the dates of the coins you find, and circle the ones that are earlier than 1965, when dimes and quarters were still made of silver. Then, all you have to do is page through that daily planner looking at the circled entries, and you will see where the best sites are for finding the older coins. Some hobbyists go so far as to keep a record sheet showing a map of where they hunted, for how long, as well as the dates of the coins they find.

Coin collecting is a popular hobby in itself. When you find old and rare coins, you'll want to see what the value is. There are books, magazines, and web sites that can help you assess the value of your collection. Some metal detecting enthusiasts simply throw all their coins into a big jar. Others like to sort and catalog them, so they can add up their total worth. Coin shops sell supplies to make short work of organizing your coins.

Many web pages can help you in your quest for knowledge about coins. See http://en.wikipedia.org/wiki/Coin_collecting. When you are at the bookstore, check out the coin collecting magazines. They will list the current values for most American coins.

B. Relics

1. The fun of relic hunting

Oh, just wait until the first time you find that cool historic relic! You'll be grinning from ear to ear. There are literally tons of awesome goodies in the ground waiting for you to discover. They range from bullets to buckles, and old toys to timepieces. They are little bits of history that tell you something about the life and times of the people who lived long ago.

Figure 22. Besides coins you'll find buckles, buttons, bullets, jewelry and other relics.

Many treasure hunters like to specialize in specific types of relics, depending on what is common in the area, and what their interests are. Civil War relic hunters are probably the most popular sub-group. There are also button historians, bottle collectors, toy enthusiasts, and all sorts of sub-specialties in relic hunting. See the following as examples:

- Bottle Collectors Haven: http://www.antiquebottles.com/.
- Collector's Connection: http://www.collectorsconnection.com/bottles.htm.
- Virginia Civil War Relics: http://www.virginiarelics.com/.

2. Common Relics

Some of the common relics you will find:

- Trade tokens were popular for businesses in the first half of the 20th century. More recent tokens include pressed pennies that are found at tourist sites, arcade game tokens, such as Chuck E. Cheese, and various vending machine tokens.
- Bullets and shell casings are common. You will find bullets from law enforcement, shooting ranges, hunters, military, and even criminal elements. Again, Civil War bullets are prized collector items.
- Buckles range from belt buckles, purse snaps, pajama clips, and horse saddle clasps.
- Buttons were sometimes made of metal. Military and Civil War buttons are important collector items.
- Toys, tin soldiers, costume jewelry
- Household items, including time pieces, nibs from ink pens, broaches, and pins
- Farm and industry items

As with coins, hobbyists have all sorts of standards regarding saving, collecting, and storing their relic finds. There is a brisk business on the internet for people who like to sell or trade the many things they find. In fact, many sellers use the term "metal detector finds" to describe the various and sundry treasures that come their way.

3. Identifying what you've found

Very often you'll find something that you think might be valuable, or interesting, but you cannot tell what it is, or what it was used for. Several of the online forums can be a help here. Simply post a picture and ask your fellow diggers what they think it is. Somewhere in the world is an expert, or at least somebody with a little more experience, who can tell you the identity of your little treasure. See also the "What is it?" forum on TreasureNet: .http://forum.treasurenet.com/index.php/board,14.0.html for further help. Look in the antiques section of the bookstore, too, and you will find all kinds of reference materials to help identify things. One great source is the reprinted *1897 Sears, Roebuck Catalogue*, Chelsea House Publishing (facsimile) for relic hunters.

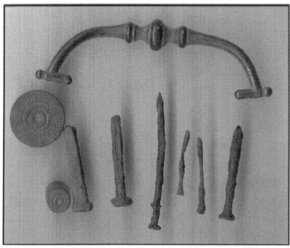

Figure 23. Square nails are a good indication you're digging in an old spot.

9. Gold Prospecting

A. Gold prospecting overview

Gold prospecting can range from a part-time curiosity for a person with a metal detector, to a full blown and distinct hobby in itself with little resemblance to the coin-shooter/treasure hunter that you'll see in a park.

Gold, silver, and other metals can be highly conductive, and display a broad range of readings on the detector display. Gold in particular benefits from a detector with higher operating frequencies. Prospecting will also steer you towards specific, often remote locations, into stream beds, and to abandoned mining areas. These factors combine to nudge the prospecting enthusiast to purchase specialized equipment.

It's true that many metal detectors have a prospecting mode that can be accessed with the simple flip of a switch, but a multiple-mode detector may not always be as well suited to the rigors of the dedicated gold prospector. The curious detectorist has at least a chance of finding microscopic traces of gold, and even an occasional nugget, but to move into the major leagues, you will need to join groups that have access to private claims, and field trips to known gold sites.

Figure 24. Gold is found with quartz rocks along the American River in California.

Hunting for gold is a different kind of experience, and requires different skills.

"Nugget hunting differs from coin-shooting. Coins are large compared to most nuggets. A one grain bit of gold is smaller than a match head and will cause a very light signal. The nugget hunter must listen for faint sounds caused by very small objects and he must train his ears for those sounds. The soil where gold is found is usually highly mineralized, so it is essential to follow the operating manual directions for tuning and ground balancing your machine."
- Dorothy B. Francis, *Metal Detecting for Treasure*

If you are interesting in exploring gold prospecting, then consider:

The Gold Prospecting Association
Internet: http://www.goldprospectors.org/
Magazine: *Gold Prospectors*
Group: Gold Prospectors Association of America, P.O. Box 891509, Tumecula, CA 92589. The association membership is separate from the magazine subscription.

You would benefit from looking at books that specialize in this subject, such as:

Recreational Gold Prospecting for Fun & Profit by Gail Butler and Paul D. Morrison (Paperback - May 1998)

Gold! Gold! How and Where to Prospect for Gold by Joseph F. Petralia, Jill Applegate, and Susan Neri (Paperback - 2006)

You Can Find Gold: With a Metal Detector by Charles Garrett and Roy Lagal (Paperback - November 1995)

B. Silver

Silver occurs in veins, just like gold. It is more difficult to identify silver than gold, as it is easily mixed up with lead or other grayish minerals. Silver will show up along a broad range of values on a discriminating detector, depending on its purity. The best bet if you think you've found a silver nugget is to bring it home and test it at a later time. The metal detecting supply stores and Internet sites sell a silver testing kit to determine if you really do have silver. The test kit uses 10% nitric acid; if the sample turns black, it is silver. This kit is handy to have for found jewelry too, as sometimes silver jewelry may be difficult to distinguish from base metals.

C. Gold-locating equipment

Since gold and silver are heavier than most rocks, they will often settle to the bottom of streams and areas where erosion has occurred. To get at it requires digging, and if this occurs in a stream there are different methods of extracting the valuable ores. Dredges, sluice boxes, and rocker boxes are tools that may be affordable for amateur prospectors, though prices can range into the thousands of dollars as the equipment gets more sophisticated. Again, gold dredging is a specialized topic. It may be too advanced to cover fully in a beginners' guidebook.

Gold also settles in cracks and crevices of bedrock, giving rise to specialized handheld equipment, such as gold probes and picks that can ferret out the fine particles.

10. Becoming a Journeyman

Once you've learned the basics of metal detecting, it's time to grow into the sport, in order to gain the maximum pleasure and rewards from your adventures. Let's look at some ways to work up to the next level.

A. Contributing and participating

There's a saying that "Friends multiply your joys and divide your sorrows." That's especially true for the people you'll meet at your local detecting club. Clubs meetings are a great place for:
- Sharing stories about your hunting trips
- Learning new techniques, learning from the pros and old-timers
- Teaching people who have less experience than yourself
- Finding bargains on metal detecting equipment
- Discovering good places to hunt
- Participating in contests and group hunts
- Meeting new friends
- Expanding your scope of activities

B. On Line Forums and Reviews

Once you've gotten your feet wet in this sport – whoa, that analogy might be a wee bit too literal! – you can more fully participate in the many online discussions available on the Internet forum web sites. You can tell others your experience with your brand of detector, and even write product reviews. You will soon become a fully engaged member of the online community. This is both a learning and a teaching experience that helps you stretch and grow, and it's a benefit to others too.

Look at all the time you spent deciding what detector to buy, and the hours you spent learning to tweak the dials. Isn't that experience valuable to people who just bought the same detector? Go on line and share your rapidly increasing knowledge.

C. Review your early choices

After you've gone on several hunts, take a few minutes to look back and re-evaluate some of your early decisions. Is the detector working the way you expected? Is that coil too heavy for your enjoyment? Is it time to buy some decent digging tools? Rather than getting into a rut that detracts from the fun, make an honest assessment of what is right and what is wrong with what you're using so far.

Apply that same evaluation process to your selection of hunting sites. Are they paying off? Would some library research improve your take-home haul? Maybe you liked going out alone, but now you find having a companion or two along with you is more enjoyable. Fellow hunters can help you improve your hunting and digging techniques, and can think of places to search you may not have thought of.

Finally, take another look at the sciences that might help you in your search for treasures. Maybe that book on geology will come in handy when you decide to look for gold nuggets. Maybe that article on ground balancing will help you adjust your detector for maximum performance.

This sport is an ongoing adventure. If you want to keep it fresh and inspiring, don't be afraid to change your mind and trek off in a new direction.

11.   Other Resources

A. The big players

The following are some of the big players in treasure hunting, as they combine a magazine and a major World Wide Web presence.

1. TreasureNet

>   Internet: http://www.treasurenet.com/
>   Forum: http://forum.treasurenet.com/index.php
>   Magazine: *Western & Eastern Treasures*

2. Lost Treasure

>   Internet: http://www.losttreasure.com/
>   Magazine: *Lost Treasure*

3. Gold Prospector's Association

>   Internet: http://www.goldprospectors.org/
>   Magazine: *Gold Prospectors*
>   Group: Gold Prospectors Association of America, P.O.
>   Box 891509, Tumecula, CA 92589.

B. Magazines

Western & Eastern Treasures
People's Publishing
P.O. Box 219
San Anselmo, CA 94979
(800) 999-9718

Lost Treasure
LostTreasure
P.O. Box 469091
Escondido, CA 92046
(866) 469-6224

Gold Prospectors
Gold Prospectors Association of America
P.O. Box 891509
Tumecula, CA 92589
(800) 551-9707

American Digger
American Digger
P.O. Box 126
Aeworth, GA 3101
(770) 362-8671

ICMJ's Prospecting and Mining Journal
ICMJ
PO Box 2260
Aptos, CA 95001
(831) 479-1500

C. Online Resources

- TreasureNet: http://www.treasurenet.com
- Lost Treasure On Line: http://www.losttreasure.com
- The Friendly Metal Detecting Forum: http://metaldetectingforum.com/index.php
- Find's Treasure Forums: http://www.findmall.com/
- Treasure Quest: http://www.treasurequestxlt.com/
- Treasure Depot: http://www.thetreasuredepot.com/index.html
- Metal Detector.com: http://www.metaldetector.cc/index.asp
- Metal Detector Reviews: http://metaldetectorreviews.net/
- Metal Detecting World: http://metaldetectingworld.com/
- Go Metal Detecting: http://gometaldetecting.com/
- Treasure Hunting: http://www.treasurehunting.com/
- Coinflation – (silver coin melt value): http://www.coinflation.com/coins/silver_coin_calculator.html
- Coin World: http://www.coinworld.com/

For **video** try YouTube or Google videos and type in "metal detecting." That will keep you entertained for quite a while! Many of the videos are instructional, and many focus on one brand, so you can learn about the equipment you have bought or intend to buy.

D. Clubs

1. National Clubs

American Metal Detecting Association Online
http://www.amdaonline.net/

The Federation of Metal Detector and Archaeological Clubs
http://www.fmdac.org/

World Wide Association of Treasure Seekers
http://www.wwats.org/

2. Lists of local clubs

For a club in your local area, see any of the links below. You can also try a search on the Internet using the keywords of your home town and the words "metal detecting club."

- Go Metal Detecting: http://gometaldetecting.com/links-clubs.htm
- Kelly Co.
          http://www.kellycodetectors.com/clubs/
- DMOZ Open Directory
          http://www.dmoz.org/Recreation/Outdoors/Metal_Detecting/Organizations/
- Friendly Forum
          http://metaldetectingforum.com/showthread.php?t=14013
- Lost Treasure
          http://losttreasure.com/clubs/index07.cfm

E. Further reading

<u>1. Books on metal detecting</u>

Detecting Metal by Fred Bonnie (Paperback – October, 1998)

The Urban Treasure Hunter: A Practical Handbook for Beginners by Michael Chaplan. (Paperback, 2004.)

The Usborne Book of Treasure Hunting (Prospecting and Treasure Hunting) by Anna Claybourne, Caroline Young, Judy Tatchell, and Jenny Tyler (Paperback – February, 1999)

Successful Treasure Hunting by Lance W. Comfort (Paperback - 2007)

The New Successful Coin Hunting by Charles Garrett (Paperback - June 1992)

You Can Find Gold: With a Metal Detector (Prospecting and Treasure Hunting) by Charles Garrett and Roy Lagal (Paperback - November 1995)

Buried Treasures You Can Find: Over 7500 Locations in All 50 States (Treasure Hunting Text) by Robert F. Marx (Paperback - Oct 1993)

Metal Detecting the Hobby by Dick Stout (Paperback - April 1993)

Coin hunting ..... in depth! by Dick Stout (Paperback - 1994)

Metal Detecting For Beginners: How to Get Started Correctly by Ed Tisdale (Paperback - 2001)

<u>2. Handy reference books</u>

Antique Tool Collectors Guide to Value, by Ronald S. Barlow (Paperback - 1999)

Collecting Costume Jewelry 101: The Basics of Starting, Building and Upgrading (Identification & Value Guide) by Julia C. Carroll (Paperback - 2004)

1897 Sears, Roebuck Catalogue, Chelsea House Publishing (facsimile; for relic hunters)

Guide to US Coins, by Coin World, (Paperback, 2009)

Antique Iron: Identification and Values, by Kathryn McNerney (Paperback – 1983)

Civil War Collector's Price Guide, by Nancy Rossbacher, (Paperback – 2000)

Standard Catalog of US Tokens, by Russell Rulau, (Paperback - September, 2004)

F. Friends and neighbors

Reminder: Your best resource for finding treasures is the people around you. Be sure to talk to neighbors, friends, family members, librarians, and historians about your interest in metal detecting. Very often older folks have stories and insight into places people congregated, or when they held outdoor social events. This is a tremendously valuable resource. All it takes is a little friendly hello, and you can steer the conversation into a discussion of your hobby. You'll be surprised how helpful and cooperative people can be.

Hint: Some treasure hunters make up a simple business card describing what they do, and have that card ready for impromptu meetings with people. Some will even carry around a few old coins to get the conversation started.

Appendix A: How a VLF Detector Works

A. VLF Technology

Take a penny, a nickel, and a dime. One by one, drop them on a desk. You'll notice each one has a distinctive clunk or clank as it bounces off the surface. With a little practice you'd soon be able to learn which coin is being dropped, even without looking. The same kind of thing happens electronically when a coin is hit with radio frequency radiation. Each coin produces a specific electronic signature which the detector can recognize. Similarly, other common items, like pull tabs, or bottle caps, have their own unique responses. Unfortunately, some common junk items have responses that are pretty close to those of valuable coins, so the detector doesn't always get it right.

The most popular instrumentation in use today is the Very Low Frequency (VLF) detector. It uses two coils, one for transmitting and the other for receiving a signal back from the search area. The receive coil is close to the transmit coil, usually concentric but smaller in size. The effects of the transmitted energy are cancelled out by running a voltage in the receiver windings in the opposite direction from the transmit coil. This balances out the magnetic field in the receive coil, which is why it is sometimes called balanced induction technology. This balancing act means any signal the receive coil detects comes from objects in the ground, rather than from the transmit coil.

The metal detector contains an oscillator, which produces an alternating current (AC) in the transmit coil. Whenever current flows in a wire it creates a magnetic field around the wire. An AC current in this coil means the current first runs in one direction, builds up to a peak, then decreases again towards zero, and repeats the same pattern in the opposite direction. The rise and fall of the voltage occurs in accordance with electrical principles to form a sine wave. Alternating current in a straight wire creates a magnetic field around it, perpendicular to the wire. When the wire is formed into the loops of the coil, this magnetic field becomes concentrated in the center of the coil, again, perpendicular to the axis of the coil. The magnetic field strength increases and decreases in time with the sine wave voltage. This means the magnetic field is continually growing then decreasing around the coil, and forms the search area of the coil.

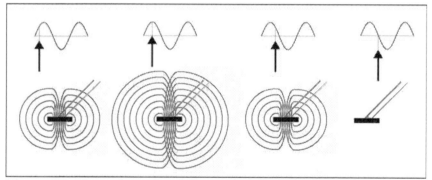

Figure 25. The voltage level for each AC cycle determines the intensity of the search field.

When such a moving field encounters a metallic object, it generates a current in that object, be it a coin, or a nail, or a bottle cap. At least, the magnetic field *tries* to create a current. Some metals, such as iron, are **resistive** to being influenced by the magnetic field. This is called ferromagnetic resistance. Other metals, such as silver, are **conductive.** They have lots of loose electrons which respond quickly to changes in the magnetic field.

The response of the target to the magnetic wave is a result of the composition of the target. It creates a **phase shift** in the received signal. Every coin or piece of metal displays some mixture of resistive and conductive properties. That mixture, the ratio of resistive to conductive makeup, will have a specific response, or signature, as picked up by the receiving coil. This enables the detector to discriminate between a coin and a piece of junk. The size of the scanned object will determine the amplitude, or loudness of the received signal. The phase shift will determine the probable composition. These two bits of information help identify the target. The output is generally fed to a meter, called a Visual Discrimination Indicator (VDI), or Target Identification (TID) circuitry, which will display a number or give a name to the target. This helps the treasure hunter decide whether to dig the target or not. Many detectors assign a number corresponding with the VDI readout. On the White's MXT metal detector, for example, the VDI for a dime might be 80, while a nickel appears as 18. After a period of working with one detector, the operator quickly learns what the numbers are for different coins and for pull-tabs.

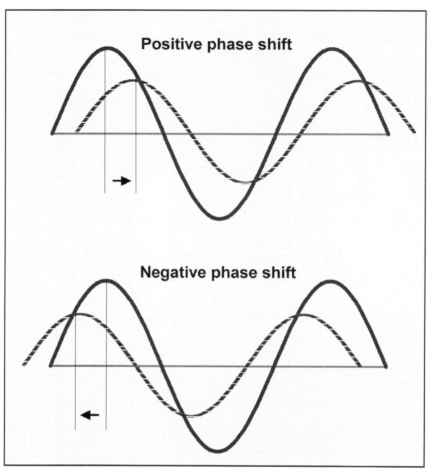

Figure 26. The composition of the target determines the phase shift in the receiver coil, dashed line, as compared to the transmit coil, solid line.

Target Identification is not always accurate. Deeper targets and coins sitting on edge are more difficult to identify. Pull tabs and other asymmetrical targets will sometimes give mixed signals depending on how you approach them. If your coil is scanning East-West, for example, a pull tab might show up as a nickel. Then when you scan it North-South it will register as a pull-tab.

Appendix B: Manufacturers and Suppliers

A. Major Brands

The major brand metal detector manufacturers generally sell detectors for land based coin, jewelry and treasure hunting, as well as specialty detectors for prospecting or underwater searching. They often sell supplies and peripherals for hobbyists.

In alphabetical order:

Bounty Hunter
1465 Henry Brennan Dr # H
El Paso, TX 79936
(915) 633-8354
(800) 444-5994
Web: http://www.detecting.com/
Bounty Hunter sells its products through major retailers, such as The Bounty Hunter Store (http://www.BountyHunterStore.com), and Kellyco, (http://www.kellycodetectors.com).

Garrett Electronics
1881 W. State Street
Garland, TX 75042
Tel: (972) 494-6151
Fax: (972) 494-1881
Web: http://www.garrett.com/
Email: sales@garrett.com
Garret has a large security division in addition to the hobby division. Charles Garrett has written several books on metal detecting.

Fisher Labs
1465-H Henry Brennan
El Paso, TX 79936
Tel: (915) 225-0333
Fax: (915) 225-0336
Web: http://www.fisherlab.com/hobby/index.htm
Email: info@fisherlab.com
Fisher Labs has three divisions, hobby, industrial, and security.

Minelab USA
871 Grier Dr., Suite B1
Las Vegas, NV 89119 USA
Tel: (702) 891-8809
Fax: (702) 891-8810
Web: http://www.minelab.com/consumer/
Email: info@minelabusa.com

Tesoro Electronics
715 White Spar Road
Prescott, AZ 86303
Tel: (928) 771-2646
Web: http://www.tesoro.com/
Email: support @ tesoro.com

White's Electronics
1011 Pleasant Valley Road
Sweet Home, OR 97386
Tel: (800) 547-6911
Fax: (541) 367-6629
White's also has regional offices around the US: See
http://whiteselectronics.com/info/contacts.html for local offices
and suppliers.

Selected Metal Detectors
Below is a selected list of coin/relic metal detectors, in alphabetical order by manufacturer. Gold prospecting and beach/underwater machines are not included in this list, as they are usually for the more advanced detectorist. The asterisks (*) designate detectors that consistently receive high user ratings, although these evaluations are changing all the time. For an up-to-date list of evaluations, I suggest Metal Detector Reviews, (on line at http://metaldetectorreviews.net/), or look at the ratings given by Kellyco (http://www.kellycodetectors.com/indexmain.php), or any of the other on line review sites. Prices are manufacturers suggest retail price (MSRP), as of June, 2009. Street prices, what you can find on sale, are generally 10% to 20% lower than MSRP.

Bounty Hunter
Quick Silver - $120
Tracker IV - $120 *
Discovery 1100 - $129 *
Lone Star - $165
Quick Draw II - $200
2200 - $210

Fisher
F2 Metal Detector - $249
1236-x2 - $400 *
F4 Metal Detector - $499
F5 Metal Detector - $549
1270x - $700 *
F70 Metal Detector - $799
1280-X - $800
ID Edge - $800
CZ-3D Target ID - $950 *
CZ-21 Target ID - $1125
F75 Metal Detector - $1199

* Detectors that consistently receive high user ratings.

Garrett

Ace 150 $180
Ace 250 - $250
GTAx 550 - $500
Master Hunter CX Plus $600 *
Master Hunter CX Plus $600 *
GTP 1350 - $700 *
GTI 1500 - $800 *
GTI 2500 - $1100

Minelab

X-Terra 305 - $495
X-Terra 30 - $495
X-Terra 505 - $695
X-Terra 50 - $695
Musketeer Advantage PRO - $895 *
X-Terra 705 - $950
X-Terra 70 - $950 *
Sovereign GT - $995 *
Safari - $1295 *
Explorer SE Professional - $1495
E-Trac - $1895

Tesoro

Compadre - $189 *
Silver uMax - $299 *
Cibola - $425 *
Golden uMax - $529
Vaquero - $550 *
DeLeon - $599
Cortes - $849

* Detectors that consistently receive high user ratings.

Whites Metal Detectors
Prizm IV - $350
Prizm V - $450
Prizm 6T - $600
M6 - $700 *
MXT $800 *
MXT 300 $900 *
Spectrum XLT - $900
DFX - $1100 *
DFX 300 - $1200 *
Spectra V3 - $1700 *

* Detectors that consistently receive high user ratings.

B. Suppliers

Suppliers, in alphabetical order:

Aardvark Metal Detectors (Distributor)
1085 Belle Avenue
Winter Springs, FL 32708
Web: http://www.aardvarkdetectors.com
Email: sales@aardvarkdetectors.com
Tel: (800) 828-1455

Accurate Locators (Manufacturer)
1383 2nd Ave.
Gold Hill, Oregon 97525
Tel: (877) 808-6200
Web: http://www.accuratelocators.com/

DetectorPro (Distributor)
Web: http://www.detectorpro.com/
Email: info@detectorpro.com
Distributor for Headhunter metal detectors and "innovative treasure hunting concepts."
See their CyberStore at
http://www.detectorpro.com/cyberstore/cyberstore1.htm

Doc's Detecting Supply (Distributor)
3740 S. Royal Crest Street
Las Vegas, Nevada 89119
Web: http://www.docsdetecting.com/
Email: cop704@yahoo.com
Tel: (800) 477-3211 Ext. 14
Distributor for Coiltek brand coils for Minelab detectors.

Famous Treasures (Distributor)
Tampa Florida
4312 Land o' Lakes
Land O' Lakes, FL 34639
Toll Free (888) 788-1819
(813) 996-1787
Email: sales@famoustreasures.com
Website: www.FamousTreasures.com

Jimmy Sierra Products (Accessories)
James and Jim Normandi
6880 Sir Francis Drake Blvd. (P.O. Box 519)
Forest Knolls, California 94933
Telephone: 1-800-457-0875
www.jimmysierra.com
jimmsierra@jimmysierra.com

JW Fishers Manufacturing (Manufacturer)
1953 County Streets
East Taunton, MA 02718
Web: http://www.jwfishers.com/
Email: info@jwfishers.com
Underwater detectors - Note: Different from Fisher Labs.

Kellyco (Distributor)
1085 Belle Ave
Winter Springs, FL 32708
Tel: (888) 535-5926
Web: http://www.kellycodetectors.com/indexmain.php
Email: orderdept@kellycodetectors.com
Note: Kellyco and other "superstore" distributors carry lesser-known brands and specialty items such as:

Automax (Pinpointing probe)
Link:
http://www.kellycodetectors.com/vibra/automaxprecisionpinpointer.htm
Cobra (Metal detector manufacturer)
Link: http://www.kellycodetectors.com/cobra/cobramain.htm
Discovery (Cache hunting metal detector)
Link:
http://www.kellycodetectors.com/cobra/vipersmain2.htm
MP Digital (Metal detector manufacturer)
Link:
http://www.kellycodetectors.com/MP3/MP3information.htm
Nautilus (Metal detector manufacturer)
Link: http://www.kellycodetectors.com/nautilus/nautilus.htm
Predator (Metal detector manufacturer)
Link:
http://www.kellycodetectors.com/cobra/vipersmain2.htm
Teknetics (Metal detector manufacturer)
Link:
http://www.kellycodetectors.com/Teknetics/teknetics.htm
Titan (Metal detectors)
Link: http://www.kellycodetectors.com/titan/titan.htm
Viper (Metal detector manufacturer)
Link:
http://www.kellycodetectors.com/cobra/vipersmain2.htm

Northwest Treasure Supply (Distributor)
P.O. Box 4212
Bellingham, Washington 98225
Tel: (800) 845-5258
Web: http://www.nwtsdetectors.com/
Email: nwts@nwtsdetectors.com

Outdoor Outfitters (Distributor)
705 Elm Street,
Waukesha WI 53186
Web: http://www.outdoorout.com/
Email: Outdoorout@ameritech.net
Tel: (800) 558 2020
Fax: 262 542 4435

Predator Tools (Digging tools)
35 South Woodruff Road
Bridgetown, NJ 08302
Web: http://www.predatortools.com/
Web: sales@predatortools.com
Tel: 856-455-3790
Fax: 856-455-6604

Simmons Scientific Products (Locating rods)
P.O. Box 10057
Wilmington, NC 28404
Web: http://www.simmonsscientificproducts.com/
Email: simmonssp@aol.com
Tel. & Fax: (910) 686-1656

Sunray Detector Electronics (In-line target probes, distributor)
106 N Main Street
P.O. Box 300
Hazleton, Iowa 50641-0300
Web: http://www.sunraydetector.com/
Email: infor@sunraydetector.com
Tel: (319) 636-2244

Appendix C: Check-list Comparison Chart

	1. ____	2. ____	3. ____
Street Price			
Discrimination			
Notch Filter			
Sensitivity			
Target ID			
Coil size(s)			
Interchangeable Coil			
Ground Balance			
Operating Freqency(s)			
Weight			
Other: ____			
Other: ____			
Other: ____			
Other: ____			
Reviews – Positive			
Reviews – Negative			
Summary			

Table 2. Fill in the chart for the top three models in your price range.

Index

13443057R00071

Made in the USA
Lexington, KY
31 January 2012